I0479618

CONTENTS

.

CHAPTER 1

Retirees in Need of Work

"I read myself out of poverty long before
I worked myself out of poverty."

Walter Anderson

Pain and Suffering

According to a 2019 story published on the website Ozy, "Why Americans Are Retiring Into Homelessness," increasing numbers of Americans over the age of 50 are ending up homeless. These are people who've worked for decades but are still ending up homeless. There's something wrong with that picture, and it's only getting worse.

A recent CNBC poll of 3,000 hourly workers from a variety of industries revealed that 40% had no savings and 75% had less than $500 saved. Although hourly workers often experience unpredictable schedules that result in erratic earnings, 40% of the survey respondents had regular work schedules.

Besides, many employers don't offer benefits (such

as insurance and retirement plans) to hourly and part-time employees. As a result, 38 million American households—25% of the workforce—live paycheck to paycheck.

People who haven't saved money don't have an emergency fund. Becoming sick or injured could easily lead to financial ruin. As a result, many people end up running up credit card debt to survive. However, the good news is that hourly employees can (and should) save money.

Because workers can't depend on employers for benefits such as a 401k, they must learn how to use their earnings to build wealth. It requires focus and diligence, but you can do it.

Living Paycheck to Paycheck

Even if you're an hourly worker who lives paycheck to paycheck, you can still save enough money to free yourself from living on the edge of ruin. Every little bit saved will give you the encouragement and confidence to save more. You may be able to seek better employment or develop new skills.

You have nothing to lose by giving the process described in this book a chance. The alternative is to become a lousy statistic—one of the people who work their whole lives only to become homeless upon retirement.

Hourly wages have stayed relatively flat over the past few decades. Payments are comparable to levels from 40 years ago. That means that it takes more money to live a comparable life. If you don't invest your money, you'll end up spinning your wheels—working on existing.

It can be OK if you're aware of it; however, most people aren't. Most people are merely existing, praying they don't have an emergency or get sick. That's a scary and stressful way to live, especially when you're working hard every day.

Change Your Current Situation

Regardless of your current status, you can change it. If you are working, you should be saving some of the money you earn. Although this book can start you on the path to building wealth, the process will require you to change your mindset.

It won't be easy.

But millions of people have done it and found a way to stop living from paycheck to paycheck. You can do it too!

The alternative is to do nothing—and that's scary. The numbers indicate that 80% of employees will retire broke. Too many people retire and rely on Social Security as their only income.

It might amount to only $18,000 a year (or $1,500 a month).

That isn't a lot of money (especially in metropolitan areas). That's why so many people retire but find they must keep working. The days of retiring and not having to work are not a reality for most people.

According to CNBC, most Americans have only $12,000 in savings when they retire, with no income other than Social Security. They are hovering on the brink of poverty, especially if there is a medical emergency that could easily wipe out savings.

You don't want that to become you. If you are working, you should have more than $12,000 by retirement.

Senior Citizen Homelessness

Because they haven't saved money, people who have worked their entire lives are ending up without the main benefit of working for all those years —a healthy retirement fund. HUD data indicate that approximately 5% of seniors aged 62 and over are homeless—and this number is growing.

AARP states that most adults aged 36-70 are financially unprepared for retirement, with most adults having no savings at all. These are the people who are relying entirely on Social Security.

However, Social Security often doesn't provide enough money to cover the necessary expenses. Most people's highest cost is rent, which increases continually. As a result, many people are forced to pay for rent at the expense of everything else—even food.

Sadly, this issue doesn't magically disappear. It is a problem that people need to solve on their own. The first step involves changing your mindset regarding money.

Imagine you had multiple streams of income that would enable you to retire without worrying about money. Wouldn't that be nice? However, this can't happen until you start investing in yourself.

Change Your Lifestyle

Reading this book is the first step in investing in yourself. You may need to change your lifestyle and how you think about money. If you don't, you stand a good chance of facing retirement and being one step away from financial ruin.

You need to realize that merely having a job doesn't mean you have money. In many cases, the situation could be an acronym for "Just Over Broke." Unless you invest the money you earn, you may become one of the senior citizens that finds themselves homeless after working for 30+ years.

Don't let this happen to you! Use the information in this book to get started on the right path. This book provides a simple plan for accumulating wealth.

Start Investing Now

Although you don't need plenty of money to start with; the most important thing is to start NOW. Regardless of whether you're 25 or 55 years old, the critical thing to know is that cash accumulates when it is saved. That's the secret—time plus money saved equals wealth.

Even if, at age 55, you started putting the maximum amount in an IRA or 401k ($7,000 per year for an IRA and $25,000 per year for a 401k), within ten years, you'd have $70,000 or $250,000 (excluding interest).

That's plenty of money—especially when you consider that most seniors have less than $12,000 in savings and depend on Social Security to get by.

If you had an additional $70,000 or $250,000 in savings, it would provide relief from stressing about money. Besides, you don't want to depend solely on Social Security or worry about becoming homeless.

Sadly, homelessness is the second biggest problem facing senior citizens, right after health issues. Homelessness among senior citizens isn't going away, especially with increasing numbers of baby boomers retiring.

Also, rising housing costs are causing people who rent rather than own homes to become homeless.

Seniors' Earning Potential

Senior citizens are particularly vulnerable because they aren't in their prime earning years, and although I say senior citizens, this statement applies to anyone over 50 years old.

The sad reality is that companies prefer to hire workers younger than 50 years old. Therefore, if you're nearing 50 years old and don't have any money saved, you need to start immediately.

This book can help you begin that process.

By the time you're 50 years old, you should have a cushion to protect against life's emergencies. This cushion helps eliminate the fear of becoming homeless in your later years. Just as there's no gain without pain, there is a pain if there is no gain.

You'll suffer later in life if you think you can get by without keeping some of your money for yourself.

Money is a Tool

After all, money is a tool. However, just like any other tool, if you don't have it when you need it, problems arise. This book is about showing you how to build wealth so that you have an ample supply of money when you need it.

Building wealth will require diligence, patience, and commitment. There's no need to change your workplace, skillset, or make more money at your job. The plan presented in this book doesn't require changes other than changing your mindset about how you use the money you currently earn.

By changing your mindset, you'll change the course of your life. You'll go from a person just working to a person working to build their wealth.

Consumerism is Eating Your Wealth

The average American earns $1,400,000 during 40 years of working from the ages of 25 to 65. That averages out to $35,000 a year. Even though this may not seem like a lot of money, it is still enough to invest some of it.

The first thing to realize is that it's not how much money you make but how much you keep. Most people don't earn a high income. However, many people with low or average incomes have been able to save more money than people with high incomes. The difference is their savings mindset.

The average income in the United States is approximately $51,000, which means that most workers should have some money to invest. However, many people have a problem with consumption.

As a result, more than a third of workers retire without any savings at all. With all the available investment vehicles, it seems like this number should be smaller. However, the problem is that everyone wants STUFF.

Buying that stuff is the reason why only 40% of workers can cover a $1,000 emergency (such as unexpected auto or home repairs).

Think about it: one-third of Americans have no savings despite working every day. The main reason they have no savings is that they overconsume because many people equate their wants with their needs.

That leads to an imbalance because the number of wants can far exceed needs. Unfortunately, many people want everything they see. However, the key is to fund only a small amount of your desires.

Buying Stuff

Consumerism accounts for 66% of the U.S. Gross Domestic Product (GDP). The economy depends on this behavior. However, it doesn't mean YOU have to abandon your wealth to buy more things.

Think of it this way. Every time you purchase something, you exchange your hard-earned money for it. If it takes you one day to make $100 and you go out and spend $100 on a fancy dinner, this means you gave up one day's worth of hard work for that meal.

Many people will say, "Well, that's why I work—to get the stuff I want." They justify it by telling their minds that their *wants* are the same as their *needs*. However, subconsciously, most people know that this is not the right decision for their financial future.

We all have a gut feeling when we are on the wrong course with our spending. We know when we are impulse buying or spending wastefully. It isn't about depriving yourself.

It IS about managing your consumption.

Because consuming just to consume is the reason

why many working people have less than $1,000 in savings.

Not having enough money saved for retirement happens because people desire a lifestyle that exceeds their earnings. They consume more than they need, and their wants end up strangling their wealth.

As they spend their future wealth on stuff, they eventually end up broke but with a lot of things. You have seen the garages filled to the ceiling with STUFF.

People who live this type of lifestyle experience despair, depression, and poverty. You don't have to become one of them.

But if you continue to consume all your earnings without thinking about the future, this will be your destiny. The goal of working is to build wealth so you don't have to work in your later years.

Otherwise, you risk ending up broke and destitute when it comes time to retire.

The Right Mindset

To turn this around, you need to have discipline, focus, and a mindset that won't allow you to over-consume. This mindset provides the resolve to help you reach your financial goals.

It is a mindset that's not influenced by advertising or what everyone else has. Instead, it is a mindset that focuses on building wealth for your future.

When you have this mindset, you're on your way to becoming wealthy. This mindset will keep you from ending up a homeless senior citizen. It will help you and your family live the best life.

Also, the right mindset will guide your decision-making. You are giving yourself the confidence to take the necessary risk to get rich.

Thinking Differently

I'm not advocating that you become super frugal and stop living your life. You can enjoy life and prepare for your future at the same time. The key is to avoid extremism in both saving *and* spending.

Most Americans have access to retirement instruments, such as a 401k or IRA. However, they aren't taking advantage of them.

Only 8% of Americans save money—so 92% don't save anything at all.

It's the biggest reason why people retire broke, homeless, or both. If you're currently in the 92% group, use this book to move to the 8% group.

It isn't hard to do, but you will have to change your mindset. You must give up some of your wants. Changing your mindset means redirecting money toward your savings and making sure you retain some of the money that you're working hard to get.

Most workers *want* to do the right thing with their

money. They know they need a better understanding of how to build wealth. The problem is they can't stop spending.

Consumer spending drives the country's economy. Everywhere you look, there's something to spend your hard-earned money on.

Unfortunately, most of this spending is because of unrelenting marketing campaigns. Advertisements are everywhere, and the average person isn't strong enough to resist the impulse to buy.

Budgets Work

One of the critical tools to prevent impulse spending is having a budget. Yes, I know you've heard this word a thousand times. Yet, most likely, you still haven't created a budget that you can do.

It's true of most people.

Only 40% of working people have a budget. The remaining 60% wing it. Yet, you are winging it with your hard-earned money and your primary tool for building your wealth.

Can you imagine a farmer taking a chance with the servicing of his tractor? That's his most important tool. He needs to make sure it is available and ready to work when needed.

So, it's hard to believe that so many people wing it when managing *their* most important tool—their hard-earned money.

Without a budget, you have no idea what's going on with your money. Looking at bank statements tells you what you spent after the fact. A budget tells you how much money you will have left after your *needs* (not your *wants*) are met.

A budget tells you how much money you will have to invest. A budget allows you to plan your investments and build a roadmap to wealth.

A budget also gives you confidence that you can reach your goals for building wealth. It allows you to see the actual flow of your money—meaning, you can change things that you don't like and keep things that you do.

A budget gives you power over your future—and it can save you from becoming an unfortunate statistic.

You must use the Information

However, a budget doesn't solve all of your financial problems; if you don't actually use the information it provides. Only having a budget isn't enough—you need to use your budget to build wealth.

That's the purpose of a budget—knowing what you spend and how you spend it. It also tells you whether you're spending money on a want or a need.

That's the main reason companies use budgets. They want to know how much money they spend

CLYDE JACK EA

and where they spend it. That information tells them how much money they are making (profits) or losing. If something is unprofitable, it gets cut from the budget.

You should be using a budget for the same reasons. If you don't run your life like a business, eventually, your finances will be in ruins. I know you don't want that to happen.

That's why you're reading this book.

You're looking for a way to prepare for your future. The remainder of this book will provide you with the tools to accomplish this goal.

16

Chapter Review

- Almost 25% of the U.S. workforce is living paycheck to paycheck. Also, nearly 80% of retirees are broke and depend on income from Social Security to live.
- As a result, more senior citizens are becoming homeless despite working for 30+ years.
- Working people are overconsuming, which keeps them from saving their hard-earned money. Ergo, many working people don't have any savings or money for retirement.
- To change this cycle, you need to run your life like a business. This involves making a budget so you can profit from your hard work and invest wisely.

CHAPTER 2

Helping Others

"Your past is important because it brought you to where you are, but as important as your past is, it is not nearly as important as the way you see your future."

Dr. Tony Campolo

Survive on Social Security

During my teens, I lived with my Aunt Bev. She relied solely on Social Security for income. Because this wasn't enough money to cover her expenses, she rented out rooms in her home, which allowed her to keep her house and pay her bills.

She may have ended up homeless, otherwise. Even though she worked her entire life, she didn't have enough money to sustain her retirement.

Most of the people Aunt Bev rented rooms to were seniors just like her. They also were trying to survive on Social Security or a small pension. In those days, most people relied on company-backed pensions for retirement.

However, the pensions were not adjusted for inflation or cost-of-living increases. As a result, many people discovered that they didn't have enough money to live on after retirement. Unfortunately, this realization didn't come until *after* retirement.

Another common occurrence was that an emergency would eat up the majority of someone's pension. It was causing many seniors to do things such as rent a room in someone's house.

Without people like my aunt, many of these seniors would have been homeless, people like Mr. Johnson.

Desperate People

Mr. Johnson was about 70 years old. Although he'd worked his entire life, he discovered that he couldn't live off his pension upon retirement. When his wife died, he got a little bit of insurance money.

However, without her financial contribution, he soon fell on hard times. He realized his choices were to live on the streets or rent a room in my aunt's house. At his age, I don't think he would have survived a year homeless.

Although he told my Aunt Bev he would only need a room for a year, he ended up staying for six years until his death. Although he didn't spend his final years homeless or starving, he did spend them worrying about money. His retirement didn't involve playing golf or sipping mint juleps on the porch.

Instead, he always worried about whether he had enough money to make it through the month.

I remember my Aunt Bev using the surplus from renting rooms to feed her tenants. The money they received covered only their most basic needs: rent, transportation, food, and clean clothes.

Many times, the roomers wouldn't have any money for food by the end of the month. So, my Aunt Bev fed them—even those who owed her money.

These people had no other place to turn when their money didn't last until the end of the month. If my aunt didn't feed them, they'd miss meals—forced to wait until they got their next check.

They hadn't done anything wrong. Most had worked for decades and hoped that their pension would be enough for retirement. Then, they retired and found out it wasn't enough. Many times, the only option was to rent rooms, like my Aunt Bev, or to get another job.

Our neighbor, Mrs. Riley, had to do just that. She retired at age 55 and was living off her pension. Then her husband got sick and couldn't work. So, Mrs. Riley had to go back to work at age 60 because her retirement wasn't enough for them.

At the time, neighborhood gossip said they were eating cat food. Whether true or not, the rumor shows how desperate things can get when there's not enough money.

Sadly, Mrs. Riley was never able to stop working after she started again. She worked almost up to the day she died at age 78.

Struggling to Survive

Getting a job wasn't an option for most of these seniors. I remember one tenant resorted to stealing things and selling them to make ends meet. He was too old to work and didn't have enough money to survive. So, he chose to become a kleptomaniac.

We had no idea until the police came looking for him. He acknowledged that it was true, but he had no other way to supplement his income. Another tenant got the extra money he needed by renting out his room in my aunt's house to others!

In other words, retirees were retiring and then going back to work. So much for being retired!

My Aunt Bev was lucky enough to be able to rent rooms to supplement her income. Who knows what would have happened if she didn't have the house? She worked for more than 30 years—just like most of her roomers.

The only problem was that they depended solely on Social Security benefits and pensions to maintain their lifestyle during their senior years.

These weren't bad people. They just weren't diligent in preparing for retirement. In their defense, there wasn't a lot of help with retirement planning like there is today. There weren't options like 401ks or IRAs. Retirement was something you did by yourself.

As a result, many seniors ended up with limited funds and few options. They didn't have investments to help them accrue wealth. That's why so many were forced to share housing or eat pet food.

Watching these seniors struggle to get by, I knew I didn't want my life to end up the same way. It became the impetus for me to learn how to invest my money. I vowed not to let their situation become mine.

Passive Income

My Aunt Bev was a savvy woman. Yet I always wondered how she was making ends meet. After all, renting rooms to destitute seniors won't make you rich, especially when many of them couldn't pay their rent on time or owed months of back rent. I knew there had to be another source of money that was helping her make ends meet.

For the longest time, I thought she was using her small savings account to subsidize shortfalls. I thought this until she fell ill and I had to write the checks for her bills. I noticed I was writing three checks for different amounts to Golden State Life Insurance and Omaha Mutual Insurance. Although the numbers weren't large, the combined payments ended up being her most significant bill.

At first, I just thought, "Wow, she pays a lot for life insurance." At the time, I didn't know anything about life insurance, but I found it interesting that these were her most significant bills. When she got better and could handle her affairs, I asked why she paid so much money for life insurance.

She said that without her life insurance policies, she would have to work or even sell her house. Being a teenager, I didn't truly understand. Thus, the next time her insurance guy stopped by, I asked him about my Aunt Bev's policies and how they helped her survive when so many others were struggling.

The salesman explained that my Aunt Bev's policies had a cash value that she could use to supplement her income. I realized that this was where the extra money came from—Aunt Bev was getting money from her life insurance policies to cover her short-falls.

I thought that was incredibly smart and savvy of my aunt. As a teenager, you usually don't think about life insurance. However, the cash value aspect was saving my aunt and me from some dire situations. It was something I didn't quickly forget.

Dying Broke

Many of our tenants and neighbors lived and died without having any life insurance. However, they could have benefitted from it, just like my Aunt Bev. Without it, they struggled to survive, and, once they died, their family struggled to find money to bury them.

Over and over, I saw firsthand how much devastation could be caused by not having a life insurance policy.

My cousin died unexpectantly at age 40. He left his wife and three kids under the age of 18 without his income. He had always seemed healthy.

However, one morning while getting ready for work, he had a fatal heart attack. Just like that, his wife and kids' lives changed immediately.

Although they mourned his sudden death, they also had to pay the funeral and burial expenses. Then they discovered that he didn't have any life insurance to cover the $10,000 for his funeral.

They ended up using their small savings account and his final paycheck—plus assistance from family and friends—to cover the funeral costs. (Back then, there were no options like GoFundMe.)

After the funeral, my cousin's wife had to sell the house because her wages couldn't maintain the home and provide for three young kids. Although the small amount of equity from the house helped give them a new start, it wasn't nearly enough.

There were plenty of times when my aunt had to help the family with groceries until the older kids could work.

I saw this scenario play out numerous times.

Several of our neighbors also had problems paying for the burials of their loved ones because there was little or no life insurance. Many times, they had to wash cars or hold bake sales to raise the money.

In some cases, people ending up taking out a loan to cover funeral expenses. That's a terrible predicament. Your loved one dies, and you must borrow money to pay for the burial.

Seeing this led me to vow that, if I ever had a family, I would protect them with life insurance.

I saw it play out again when an uncle had a sudden stroke. He lingered in the hospital for almost two months before dying.

During that time, there were murmurings about whether he had life insurance. Once he died, those murmurings became a reality.

Although he had lived a stable middle-class life—with a house and two cars in a nice neighborhood—my uncle didn't have enough insurance to cover the costs of his funeral.

My aunt had to figure out how to make things work. Just like my cousin's wife, she ended up selling her home and other items to get by. If my uncle had more life insurance, my aunt probably could have kept their home.

Become Prepared

My uncle and cousin worked every day. They both

knew about life insurance. Heck, my uncle even had a small policy. However, they didn't understand how insurance works.

My Aunt Bev understood how insurance worked, which is why she was able to use the cash value from her policies to supplement her income. She also knew that once she died, her accounts would have enough money to bury her and help her beneficiaries.

That's what happened.

When Aunt Bev passed away at the age of 80, her life insurance policies covered all her expenses. There was no need for car washes or bake sales. We had a good time remembering her for who she was and not worrying about paying her debts.

After seeing what happened with my cousin and uncle, I was glad that my aunt prepared.

After those experiences, I knew that I needed life insurance. At first, I got a term insurance policy because the premium was only $25 monthly for $200,000. Eventually, I could afford a whole life policy.

This policy is now accumulating cash value, just like my Aunt Bev's policy. If I ever need it, I will have it at my disposal.

Aunt Bev had always said that you need some money for a rainy day. Life insurance was her way of having that money. After seeing the pain and suffering caused by not having a policy, why would anyone want to put their family through that turmoil during their time of grieving?

You don't want that to happen to your family. I knew I didn't want it for my family.

Think and Grow Rich

That's why I decided to find a way to get rich.

I read all the top books on getting rich: Think and Grow Rich, The Millionaire Next Door, The Richest Man in Babylon, How to Think Like a Millionaire.

I was seeking the knowledge I knew I would need to succeed at my goal. To get rich. I didn't want to live a life of constant financial struggle. I saw how that life left all those involved broke and miserable.

That drove me to want to get rich so bad that I could see nothing but that as my goal. I was starting with no money. It caused me to stress about how I would reach my goal, but I kept looking for a way to get on a path towards getting rich.

Eventually, A co-worker introduced me to mutual funds, which were becoming popular. He told me he was allowing the mutual fund company to withdraw funds from his account monthly automatically. He further explained how mutual funds worked. I was intrigued to learn more about mutual funds.

So, I visited the library, because this was the cheapest way to learn about mutual funds and investing, period. Otherwise, you would have to subscribe to an industry paper like the Wall Street Journal, Investor's Business Daily, or Barron's, and these subscriptions weren't cheap. At the library I could read theirs for free. Also, I could access even more information on a mutual fund through the library's microfiche.

Now that I had found my access to quickly accumulating wealth, I just needed a plan—one that would help me become rich, even if it took thirty years.

Making Money

Eventually, I invested in T Rowe Price and Neuberger Berman, putting $3,000 in T Rowe's Mid-cap growth fund and $2,000 in Neuberger Berman's growth fund.

That was the beginning of my investing for wealth. Throughout this time, 401(k) and IRA vehicles weren't as popular as they are now.

Most mutual funds were risky, even though they were leading the market as the instrument offering the best returns—and, ultimately, they became the instrument for most individual investors and retirees, which helped these products to grow.

Due to my knowledge of mutual funds and my increased need to get rich via investing, I set up these accounts to automatically withdraw a few hundred dollars per month from my bank account.

Just as my co-worker had stated, this arrangement allowed me to "set it and forget it."

I didn't have to remember to send in a deposit—it was transacted automatically. That was of great benefit to me because I wasn't disciplined enough to stay consistent.

With this arrangement in place, plus replacing my term policy with a whole life policy, I had found a path to getting rich.

Eventually, these two assets helped me save over $6,000 per year, which accumulated into over $100,000 in ten years. I used this money to finance my future investing.

Losing

Thus, I became a student of investing in mutual funds. I used the industry papers, and I attended investor conventions. I learned how to buy low-cost mutual funds and how to transition from a bull to a bear market by using money market accounts.

Even with all that new knowledge, I wasn't ready for what was about to happen: The market crashed in 1987.

I lost 80% of my investment.

Mainly because the crash was sudden and deadly, there wasn't enough time to transfer money to my money market account.

Being naive, I thought all investing was that easy:

just invest your money and watch it grow. Well, this debacle sent me running to preserve my remaining funds.

I was sick to my stomach for months. I didn't have that type of money to lose; I was a working person.

Even after the disastrous losses from the Black Monday crash, I still knew I could make money investing my money.

I knew I had to keep trying. That's a mantra I told myself almost daily.

Chapter Review

- Social security income isn't enough to depend on in retirement
- More workers are retiring broke and homeless
- Having a whole/universal life insurance policy is a necessity for working people
- You must become active in your retirement plan—passive income equals supplemental income

CHAPTER 3

Secrets to Getting Rich

"One man has enthusiasm for 30 minutes; another has it for 30 days. But it's the man who has it for 30 years who makes a success of his life."

–Edward Butler

The goal of this book is to have readers take action to increase their wealth and live their best lives. However, there are secrets to learn—secrets that are the backbone of accruing wealth. If you use these secrets, your path to getting rich will be more natural.

Enthusiastic Thinking

After my youthful experience with the desperation caused by not having enough money, I vowed never to become a statistic. If I lived long enough, I didn't want to retire and still must work to survive. To do this, I knew I had to change my views about money.

The mindset described by Edward Butler—30 years

of enthusiasm—is necessary for getting rich. I know this sounds like a lot of time, primarily when most people can't focus for longer than a minute.

Many people want to barely get by, and that's OK. However, they probably won't become rich. It is the person who wants to do more than get by who needs this mindset. These people will have to make sacrifices while they build wealth. It won't be easy, but you can do it. You need to commit.

Emmitt Fox once said: "Whatever you persistently allow to occupy your mind will magnify in your life."

Meaning that if you occupy your thoughts with the idea of accumulating wealth, that will become bigger in your life.

In his classic book *Think and Grow Rich*, Napoleon Hill said: "Thoughts are things, and powerful things at that, when they combined with definiteness of purpose, persistence, and a burning desire for their translation into riches or other material objects."

These quotes demonstrate the power of thoughts and having the proper mindset. Your mindset should be like the tortoise in *The Tortoise and the Hare*. The tortoise had a strong desire to complete his goal. He didn't worry about losing to the hare— he only wanted to reach the finish line.

The moral of that story was "slow and steady win

the race." You should have this same mindset when building wealth. Take it slow and steady, and you will eventually reach your goal.

The Right Environment

Wealth isn't just money. If you have money and no health, you're in trouble. Wealth means being rich in all areas—health, spirituality, and money. Although this book is about increasing your monetary riches, you need good health to maintain the right mindset.

After all, it is challenging to try to get rich while dealing with health problems. It is also impossible to be enthusiastic when you're sick. Maintaining your physical and mental health helps maintain the right mindset. After all, your mindset drives your energies toward your goal, which will ultimately result in monetary wealth.

A healthy lifestyle isn't just what you eat or drink. It also requires your environment to be healthy. You can't be around people who aren't after the same thing.

The right environment is critical. It's already tough to get rich when you're starting with nothing. Add in a negative atmosphere that doesn't support your goals, and you'll have an even tougher time. A healthy environment makes your success easier and faster, which is why you must be aware of your surroundings.

This awareness will help you maintain a healthy life, which is a factor in getting rich. Without good health, you won't be able to maintain your enthusiasm for 30 years.

Desire

Your desire to build wealth must be strong enough that it forces you to succeed because that's the only way to meet your goal. This is especially true if you're coming from no money.

I started with no money. I can tell you that, if you want to be rich, you can do it—it is within your reach. Having the right mindset will keep you focused and consistent, which will encourage you to seek information on achieving your goal.

Your mindset will also help you make sacrifices to achieve your goal. For example, you'll be able to go a month without eating out or will give up a planned trip. In other words, you'll be willing to give up the things that prevent you from saving and investing your money.

However, you won't need to sacrifice much, If you avoid one "want" and invest that money, you'll become more prosperous.

For example, suppose you're spending $400 every month on entertainment. If you cut that amount in half, you'll have $200 a month to invest. In five years, that money can grow to $12,000, excluding interest. You accumulated that money because you reduced the cost of a want!

You don't have to give up your life and become a hermit to get rich. However, you will need to make sacrifices—give up some of your wants—and invest that money. To do this, try reducing some of the money you spend on desires. *That's* the type of mindset you need!

Having Patience

Building wealth takes time. That's why you need patience, especially if you're starting with little money. It's not about getting rich quick. Having the right mindset will provide you with the endurance you need to build wealth over time.

To do this, you must transition from a "wishing mind" to a "doing mind." It'll require you to recondition your thinking. You can do this by studying. Your newfound knowledge will then make it possible to act, which is the mindset of a doer.

You will no longer be merely wishing for dreams and goals— you'll make them happen instead. This change will be the fuel that propels your success. Once you retrain your mind to "do" instead of "wish," investing becomes easier.

Focusing on and studying investing retrains your mind so that both your subconscious and conscious mind stay focused on your goal. For example, when I wasn't reading about investing or researching investments, I used positive affirmations to focus on my goals. Doing this helps you stay focused without deviating from your plan.

You won't have to spend a lot of time. It just requires you to be aware of your priorities. Focusing on investing and saving money will make them a priority in your life and will keep you focused on your long-term goals.

An hour of studying each day is more than enough time to retrain your mind. After all, you don't want to get overloaded with too much information.

As Zig Ziglar once said, "Repetition is the mother of learning, the father of action, which makes it the architect of accomplishment."

You Can Do It, If You Try

When you have the right mindset, you can focus on a goal for 30 years and see it come to fruition. This mindset will get you rich. Remember that whatever you tell yourself is what is going to happen. Our entire lives revolve around what we tell ourselves. If you think you can do it, you will.

Most people give up on their goal of getting rich too soon. These people won't become rich because they aren't mentally ready and don't have the right mindset.

With the right mindset, investing and making money becomes more natural. Once you establish your goals, adopt a laser-like focus on reaching them; nothing should get in the way. Doing this will minimize distractions and the noise in your head. Once the madness is gone, you can focus on building wealth.

This clarity will keep you from giving up and will empower you to seek the knowledge that you need. In other words, the right mindset allows you to withstand negative setbacks and invest with confidence.

"Financially independent people are happier than those in their same income/age cohort who are not financially secure."

–The Millionaire Next Door

Foundational Wealth

Once you have the right mindset, you need to build a financial foundation. Without preparing a foundation, you're creating a fortune that's unprotected. After all, you wouldn't build a house without first laying the foundation. The same applies when investing. The first investments you make should establish your financial foundation.

Establishing a foundation *before* building your fortune protects your assets from the unexpected. A good foundation keeps your assets from being tied up in courts and taken by lawyers. Don't build wealth without protecting it as it grows.

Several instruments can protect your investments

from taxes, liabilities, and death, including LLCs, S Corps, living trusts, wills, and life insurance. Wealthy people use these instruments to reduce risk, limit taxes, and provide for loved ones. You should use them for the same reasons.

Many people think these types of instruments aren't for them or will cost money they don't have. This type of thinking usually causes more grief in the long run, which is what you're trying to avoid. The bottom line is that you need some of these instruments to protect your investments.

Legacy

To ensure your wealth will last, you must structure it for posterity. Living trusts, life insurance, corporations, and LLCs are all used for this purpose. They will protect your fortune. With the proper tools, one million dollars can provide for ten generations. The key is how you set up the money.

A trust can dictate how long your fortune lasts. For example, you might place a property in a trust and say that it can't be sold until ten years after your death. Instructions like this will ensure that your goals are carried out after your death.

Using these instruments also guarantees that your family—not lawyers—benefits from your wealth. Therefore, you need to protect and preserve your wealth. Otherwise, it will go to probate.

We've all heard about celebrities whose estates

were lost because they didn't adequately protect their assets. In these cases, the people that the stars wanted to benefit from their fortunes ended up with nothing. In some circumstances, entire estates vanish.

Setting up your estate for future generations guarantees that your wealth benefits the people and organizations *you* want to support—not what a court decides. By carefully structuring your wealth, it can outlast you and future generations.

One common scenario is when a benefactor distributes wealth in a staggered plan. For example, if the estate is for 1 million dollars and the benefactor wants it to last for 20 years, the estate must be structured to pay out only $50,000 per year. This way, the benefactor's money lasts longer, and the beneficiary has the security of knowing they will receive money every year.

Sometimes, benefactors have insurance policies that go into a trust that dictates how the proceeds get distributed. Although you don't *have* to put insurance policies in a trust to avoid probate, this might be a good option if you want to dictate how the money gets used.

Otherwise, upon your death, the beneficiaries will receive the proceeds in a lump sum, which could be disastrous.

You can even place limited liability companies (LLCs) into a trust and dictate how the LLC will run. All these options give you power after death to determine how your hard-earned money works for the betterment of others, ensuring that your legacy reflects who you are and will be your voice for years to come.

Helping Others

An AARP poll found that 42% of baby boomers and 64% of Generation Xers don't have a will or living trust. If they died today, their estate would probably go to probate. Their beneficiaries would be lucky to see any of it.

To build a foundation, you need two main instruments: a living trust and life insurance. A living trust protects your assets in life and death. Life insurance protects your loved ones in the event of your untimely death.

Both instruments guarantee that your loved ones—not attorneys or court-appointed executors—benefit from your wealth. Many families have lost their wealth because they didn't have these instruments in their portfolio.

Estate planning is about protecting your beneficiaries. The foundation of your financial plan must include these protections; you should establish this before you start investing.

Many great industrialists of the past left legacies, including the Carnegie, Duke, and Vanderbilt families. Although they have been dead for years, their legacy lives on. They are still determining how their wealth gets spent, even after all these years. They live on via the trusts they established.

You can do the same thing—structure your wealth for posterity through trust and life insurance. That'll help it last beyond one generation. Although you can do this with any amount of money, it helps if you have a large amount.

Part of your money should go to outside charities. Although there are too many to name, many excellent charities help people when times are tough. The key is to find one that you like and share your money with it, using your legacy to affect change in the lives of the less fortunate.

The message I'm trying to convey is that your legacy should help people who aren't your direct family. Although you can give to whomever you want, giving all your money to your family isn't as fulfilling as helping a stranger.

Building a legacy that helps the needy benefits society—the society that helped you earn money in the first place. Yes, you read that right. You need things to go well in your community for your investments to accrue wealth.

Your legacy is a lasting tribute to your efforts and will live on after you. You should be humble in this process because helping others is truly amazing. The effect of giving blesses you with more.

Remember, you can't physically take it with you,

but you can benefit spiritually. By giving, your spirit feels happier and lighter. There is less weight on your soul every time you help someone else.

Therefore, begin your journey to building wealth by establishing a financial foundation that ensures your legacy. You should do this first because it gets more expensive and complicated as you get older.

Also, if you put it off, it might not get done at all. Then, if the unexpected happens, it will be too late. Although this sounds scary, it happens more often than you think.

Chapter Review

- Your thinking determines your success
- You must be patient with yourself when trying to achieve a goal
- Unlimited enthusiasm is required to get rich
- What will your legacy be?

CHAPTER 4

Working Person Investments

"Unless you try to do something beyond what you have already mastered, you will never grow."

—*Ralph Waldo Emerson*

Investing in Getting Rich

You can invest in a wide variety of things—from extreme investments, such as exotic birds, to more traditional investments, such as stocks, bonds, and real estate.

Most extreme investments only make money for a select few. Breeding horses is one such example. This investment often experiences losses that are unsustainable for the novice.

In this chapter, I'm going to provide an overview of standard investment instruments. Because I can't go into detail about each investment, you will need to conduct further research before investing in any of these instruments.

There are two types of investments: passive and active.

Passive investing is when you don't actively participate in the investment. You purchase the investment and let it do its thing. An example would be your IRA. You put money into the account and let it accumulate—there's no other involvement on your part.

Active investing means you actively participate in the investment. An example would be managing real estate rentals. You can have both passive and active investments in your portfolio. The key is to choose the investments that are best for you.

Most millionaires got rich through passive investing. And initially, you should do the same. You don't have to reinvent the wheel. It's a proven process. All you have to do is follow the same steps they used to get rich.

Investments that Work

As I mentioned earlier, there is a myriad of things you can invest your money in, from the exotic (animals) to the standard (stocks). With these types of options, the average working person who is trying to get rich becomes confused.

And when confusion is their guide, they usually make the wrong decision, buying a losing investment over a good one.

I had two clients who were coworkers. One of them

was that type of person. He would allow public hysteria to determine his investing decisions.

When chia pets were popular, he invested and lost. Then beanie bear came along, and once again, more money was lost chasing fads.

His coworker was investing in the company's 401(k) plan, for which the company provided a matching contribution of 3%. After 22 years, he had accumulated over $500,000. And he was only 47 years old.

His fad-chasing co-worker barely had $50,000 in his 401(k) after 16 years on the job.

Don't chase investments that are fads or exotic when you could invest in an investment that is proven to work. You are losing wealth by chasing the unknown.

Some investments are proven to make a working person wealthy. These investments have helped others do the same, me included. You should begin with these investments first.

They are the basis of your investing foundation, and they are easier to understand than "Chia Pets" or "Beanie Babies."

The Best Investment for You

There are a lot of investments, especially if you have the money. You could have exotic animals and stocks or mansions and a lot of cars. All these things are possible with money.

But if you don't have any money to start, as a working person, your menu of assets to invest in is limited. And that's okay because, if you use the tools that are available to you, eventually, you will be able to invest in those other things.

There are some investments made for a working person that is trying to get rich.

Here are the three best investments for working people:

1. Life insurance (a cash value policy)
2. IRA/401(k)
3. Personal home

These investments are all set up to benefit you personally with tax benefits. Each of them either helps you to reduce your taxes, defer your taxes, or implement a tax-free distribution.

There are no other investments, at your level, that can offer you the same tax benefits, which is why you must use these investment vehicles to their fullest.

They will most definitely make you wealthy. And, help your legacy last into posterity.

Below is an overview of these investments and how they can benefit your wealth-generating goal.

*"A journey of a thousand miles
begins with a single step."*

—Lao Tzu

Life Insurance

The essential item in your foundation is a life insurance policy. Whether it's term, universal, or whole life insurance, it is crucial to have life insurance, especially if you have children.

If you die, your family could be in danger because your assets may have to be liquidated to pay off your debts—leaving nothing for them.

That is what happened to my cousin. His family ended up with nothing. I'm sure this isn't what you want for your loved ones.

Although most investors are taught to invest in stocks and mutual funds, they would do themselves and their families a lot of good by investing in life insurance first. That's why the big banks invest in life insurance.

Life insurance can be a conservative but consistent investment. It also offers tax benefits you don't receive when investing in stocks and mutual funds. That's not to say those types of investments aren't suitable.

However, they should come *after* you obtain a life insurance policy to protect your family's future. Once you have a life insurance policy in place, then you should invest in the other assets.

There are three types of life insurance to consider:

term life insurance, whole life insurance, and universal life insurance. There are benefits and drawbacks to all three. For a deeper understanding of these products, consult an insurance agent for specifics.

The fundamental differences are below.

Term life insurance is for a limited time, such as 5, 10, or 20 years. When the term is up, you can forego coverage or get coverage with different payments.

Term life insurance is typically less expensive and is the most popular choice for most people.

However, each time a term ends, you need to get new insurance, which means a different rate. People use term insurance to have something. It is best for those just starting and who need insurance to provide for their families.

Whole life insurance is guaranteed to remain in force for the life of the insured (hence the name) — the type of policy my Aunt Bev had.

The premiums are much higher than term insurance and are fixed payments. (This is unlike term insurance, which gives you a new payment amount every time you get a new policy.)

There is also a cash value component to a whole life policy, which functions like a savings account for the policyholder. In most cases, you can access this cash without paying taxes.

A universal life policy is like a whole life policy in

that it has a cash value component. The big difference is that the cash value generates interest, tied to a financial index (such as stocks and bonds).

You can access the premiums you paid if you have a whole or universal life insurance policy. You could use that money for retirement or other things. This cash can be accessed tax-free at any age.

Unlike IRAs, there are no penalties for using the money.

Both types of policies offer interest on your premium, which can be higher than what you can get via the stock market. That's the reason why banks and corporations place millions of dollars into these types of policies. It is difficult to find an investment that offers a better return-to-risk scenario.

Some insurance agents will present all three types of insurance policies. If you select term insurance for the cheaper premiums, they'll advise you to invest the difference.

However, the average person won't consistently invest that money, which is the biggest problem with that advice.

With a whole/universal life insurance policy, your money is already being invested, even though you're paying a higher monthly premium. There is nothing for you to remember to do. And most of the time, the returns will be better than you could get if you tried to invest the difference.

Not only do you have the policy to protect your family, but you also get the benefit of investing your money and being able to access it.

However, even if you opt not to get a whole life or universal life insurance policy, be sure to get term life insurance. You would still be providing your loved ones with some assistance should you die.

IRA/401K

Most workers look forward to retirement. They envision having time to do whatever they want without worrying about money. Individual Retirement Accounts (IRAs) and 401ks are the number-one vehicle used for that purpose.

I'll discuss the two types of IRAs first and then look at 401ks.

It is critical to maximize your contributions to an IRA because of the tax benefits. Contributions to a traditional IRA reduce your taxable income via a deduction, which may lower your tax bracket.

With a traditional IRA, you delay paying taxes on that income until you withdraw the money. Mandatory withdrawals begin at the age of 70.5. The idea is that your taxable income will be lower at this age, therefore reducing your tax bracket. In most cases, this ends up being true.

However, there are penalties for early withdrawals, which usually are about 10% of the amount you withdraw. The only exceptions are if you use the monies to purchase a primary residence or must go on permanent disability.

A Roth IRA also allows you to grow your retirement money, but you don't have to pay taxes upon withdrawal because you pay the taxes upfront. This is another difference from traditional IRAs because contributions to Roth IRAs aren't tax-deductible.

However, with a Roth IRA, you can withdraw contributions at any time without penalty or paying taxes.

Just be sure to consult the 5-year rule if you're considering withdrawing any monies. To help you determine if your withdrawals will be free of penalties and taxes.

Regardless of whether you have a traditional or Roth IRA, both tools help fuel your investment returns, with the added benefit of offering either tax-deferred or tax-free withdrawals. You should have at least one of these tools in your portfolio.

The maximum contribution for IRAs is $6,000 for under age 50 and $7000 for age 50+. After 20 years of maximum contributions, you would have saved $120,000 to $140,000, excluding accrued interest. This averages out to $20 per day.

Most likely, you waste this amount on frivolous things. As you can see, a little money can add up quickly and, when invested correctly, can become the wealth you need in later years.

The key is finding the discipline to make that maximum contribution consistently.

"If you can get up the courage to begin, you have the courage to succeed."

David Viscott

The beauty of a 401(k) is that some employers match employee contributions. Just like a traditional IRA, the deposits are tax-deferred until withdrawal. Because they are deducted from your paycheck before taxes, contributing to a 401(k) also helps reduce your taxable income.

The other good thing about a 401(k) is that you can contribute a maximum amount of $19,000 a year (or $25,000 for ages 50+). That's a lot of deferred money for a working person! If your employer matches that amount, you could save up to $38,000 yearly. However, the average employee match percentage is 6% of what you invest. For $19,000, that's an additional $1,100 from your employer.

If you work at a job that has 401k employer matching, sign up immediately to take advantage of this benefit. Even if your employer doesn't match contributions, you should still enroll in that plan.

Eventually, it could be the money that fuels your other ventures, such as buying your primary home.

The benefits offered aren't found in any other retirement vehicle. That's why they are the best investments for working people to invest in for retirement. They were set up to give you an added benefit to save: tax relief. When a working person doesn't take advantage of these investment vehicles, they are losing money.

Even if you can't deposit the maximum, you should still contribute whatever you can. It'll help reduce your taxable income.

I've often heard people say it's not good to invest in a company's 401k plan. If you ask them why, they often can't provide a good enough reason to justify their belief—other than the myth that 401ks are a conservative investment.

This isn't true. You get to select the mutual fund for your money. Therefore, if you are aggressive, you can choose aggressive funds. What these naysayers are missing is that this is the best vehicle for working people with little money to invest. It's set up to benefit them.

There's not a better investment to make if you are a working person trying to get rich other than buying a personal residence.

You should make sure you contribute to this investment every year; even if you it's not the maximum amount, send something. Try to make deposits for ten years, you will be thankful you did.

Personal Home

The most popular way to invest in real estate is to purchase a primary home. If you don't own a home, you should make that your first real estate investment. The benefits—aside from providing stability for you and your family—are many.

However, the most significant benefit is that you build equity with each payment. If there's appreciation, you get that, as well. If you're savvy, you can use that equity to build your wealth.

Owning a home helps reduce the cost of living. As a renter, you never know when the rent will go up, if the place you live in will become undesirable, or if the owner will sell. Any of these options can create instability for your family.

When buying a home, most people get a fixed-rate mortgage, which means they make fixed monthly payments for a set number of years (usually 30). This length of time typically encompasses your working career. At the end of this time, your home should be paid off.

Then, if you choose to retire, you won't have mortgage payments, which frees up your cash flow. The freed-up cash can be invested to make money or to help with your lifestyle. And, of course, you have equity available to enrich your life and your investment opportunities further.

Another benefit of owning a home is that the fixed payments help with budgeting and planning your wealth-building goals. If you have any surplus left from your earnings, you can invest it.

It doesn't matter how small the amount is—every little bit count.

Even if you save only $200 a month, you can put it into a mutual fund account. Then, in 20 years, you would have $48,000 (excluding gains). All this would accumulate just from saving $200 monthly.

I know this doesn't sound like a lot of money, but whenever your money earns money, you build wealth.

Owning your residence is essential to all your future investments. It helps you get financing from banks—whether you use the equity or put the house up as collateral.

In general, banks are more apt to fund other investments when you own a home. You also could use the equity in your home to buy a business.

Plus, there's a tax benefit to owning your own home. You can still deduct your mortgage interest.

Never use the equity in your home for frivolous things, though. You shouldn't use the capital if you're unsure about an investment's ability to return the principal.

Always do your homework and be confident that your investment dollars are safe. Although nothing is guaranteed, you can increase the odds of success by doing your homework.

The most important reason to own a home is that

you will always need a place to live. That security gives you the stability to grow and invest.

When you rent, you can't be an investor because renting is a losing investment. Every time you write a check, you lose that money.

If you are paying $1,000 monthly, that's $12,000 a year—that is a lot of money for a working person! If you multiply that by five years (which is the average amount of time renters stay in a place), you've given up $60,000 to a landlord.

You can't be an investor and lose that type of money.

In other words, you won't get rich by renting. If anything, that's how you stay broke. The only time there's nothing wrong with renters is if you own the property!

Living Trust

After you have invested in these best investments for working people, you should consider setting up a living trust. Such is true, especially if you are going to invest in other assets.

You don't need it for your life insurance and retirement accounts. But your house, cars, and other investments should be in trust.

A living trust is a legal document that specifies how you want to manage your assets while you are alive and after your death. If you set up a living trust for your assets, you are called the "grantor" or "settlor." Whoever you elect to manage the assets is called the "trustee."

There are two types of living trusts. A revocable living trust is when you transfer your assets into the trust and retain control of those assets as the trustee. You elect yourself to be the "trustee" and name a successor to take over upon your death.

You can change or revoke the trust whenever you want. Upon your death, all assets will pass to your beneficiaries without going to probate. One thing a revocable trust *can't* do is protect your assets from creditors. If a creditor wins a lawsuit against you, they can pursue the assets.

An irrevocable trust allows for the permanent distribution of your assets. When selecting this type of trust, your assets are no longer under your control and your estate.

The benefit is that your assets aren't subject to estate taxes, and creditors can't come after this type of trust. However, you do give up control over the assets.

It's best to consult with an attorney or an online resource (such as LegalZoom) before setting up a living trust. The cost to set up a living trust can range from $500 to $5,000.

If you don't have a lot of items to include in your trust, a living trust can be easy to set up yourself. If you have a primary residence, some family heirlooms, personal vehicles, and bank accounts, then you can use a "do-it-yourself" service like Legal-Zoom.

But if you have a lot of property, other than the basics, you will need an attorney to establish your living trust. Although using an attorney will cost more, you don't want to skimp on protecting your most valued assets.

The reason I recommend using a living trust instead of a will is that a will becomes effective after death when it goes into probate. Probate can be time-consuming and costly. It is when lawyers come into play.

A living trust completely avoids probate. The successor trustee of your living trust carries out your instructions as documented.

Also, because a living trust is a "living" document, it allows you to administer it while you are alive. If you become incapacitated, it will become your voice for financial, healthcare, and legal affairs.

The biggest reason people use trusts is to avoid probate. Probate is a legal process that distributes your assets according to a will or if you die intestate (without a will). Probate can take months (or even years), depending on the size of the estate or if beneficiaries contest the will.

Also, the contents of a will become public record. If you like your privacy and don't want your hard-earned money going to lawyers, then it is best to establish a living trust.

Once the beneficiaries get the assets, the living trust ceases to exist. There are no lawyers or court fees to be paid. The recipients will be happy you had a living trust.

You really can't lose by establishing a living trust. It's the ultimate probate avoidance tool. The rich have been using these instruments for years to control and protect their assets. (This is where the phrase "trust fund baby" comes from.)

A living trust provides you with peace of mind in knowing that your wishes will be carried out in life and on your death. Don't start building your assets without getting protection for those assets and your beneficiaries.

Initially, I didn't have a living trust because I didn't know much about them or that they were so easy to form. It seemed like it was something for people with a lot of assets—not a person just starting. When I took the leap, I used LegalZoom. And, I had an attorney review the document to make sure that everything was okay.

Great Possibilities

If you want to get wealthy as a working person, it's doable, even if you are starting with no money. That's what these investments do.

I used all these investments to help me get rich, and

you can do the same.

Remember, they were set up expressly for your benefit: to help working people accrue wealth.

So if you aren't using these investment vehicles, then you are losing money. And, that's money you can't afford to lose. Particularly, if you don't have a company or municipal pension, you can benefit.

As I mentioned, the future looks bleak for workers who are depending solely on social security. The homeless ranks are filling up with seniors who can't afford to live after retiring. Yet, most of them worked all their lives.

Still, they ended up homeless or eating pet food. This is all because they didn't take advantage of these vehicles to wealth.

If you are working and still have some years left before your retirement, you had better take advantage of either an IRA or a 401(k), if they are available. Otherwise, you may have to work until you die.

These instruments open great possibilities for you. They offer you the chance to go from being broke, like I was, to becoming wealthy. These instruments have provided my family and me a life devoid of money problems.

Chapter Review

- Don't chase fads masked as investments.
- There are only three investments created for working people.
- Having a living trust is integral to your wealth-building.
- Using these three best investments will make you rich

CHAPTER 5

Just Do It

"The great use of life is to spend it for something that will outlast it."

William James

Most people get stressed when they think about investing or saving money, mainly because of the myriad options available to them. They become mentally paralyzed and don't do anything, even though they know this isn't the right approach.

This mental paralysis consists of fear. Most are afraid of making a mistake and losing money. So, you do nothing. If you do nothing, it leaves you with nothing at retirement.

That's why you must do something, even if it's the bare minimum, which can still be a lot.

There are instruments available for you to safely grow your money. Listed are some simple plans to help with your investing goals. The key to these plans is that you must allow the funds to be withdrawn automatically, without interruption.

Eventually, you won't even notice that money until you read a statement. Always remember that you are building wealth so you can have multiple sources of income upon your retirement. Your needs won't depend solely on Social Security checks.

Plan #1: IRA/401(k) Investing

There are two benefits to using this plan: tax-deferred and tax deduction. Both provide you with a win/win opportunity.

With a 401(k), there's also the possibility to get a matching contribution from your employer.

Wow! You can't beat these benefits.

This is especially true if you can invest up to $7,000 in an IRA and up to $25,000 in a 401(k). This will all be tax-deferred, and it'll help reduce your taxable income by the amount you have invested. (IRA contributions are $6,000 for under 50 years old/$7,000 for 50+, and 401(k) contributions are $19,000 for under 50 years old/$25,000 for 50+.)

You should always fund your 401(k) before you fund any other investment account.

For instance, if you are grossing $50,000 and invest $7,000 in an IRA, your taxable income will now be $43,000. Or if you put $25,000 in a 401(k), your taxable income would be $25,000. That's additional money you could use. A reduction benefits you tremendously if you reinvest the savings. These types of moves will make you wealthy.

Your monthly investment will need to be around $580–$2100, depending on whether it's an IRA/401(k). These amounts are for funding the max contribution. It may seem like a lot of money, but it's doable, especially if you allow automatic withdrawals from your checking or bank account. You won't have the pressure of remembering to invest the money. It's the out of sight, out of mind theory.

Now, don't become discouraged by these numbers. Remember, these are the max amounts that you can put into these accounts. You can always contribute less. The initial main objective should be to start investing whatever you can. So, if you need to start with half of that amount, $291-$1000 monthly, that's okay. Your goal is to start somewhere.

If you do this for five years, your account will have $17,000-$60,000, excluding interest earned depending on whether it's an IRA or 401(k). And, in 30 years, if you have that amount of time, your account balance would be anywhere from $102,000-$360,000. You can achieve this type of investing success with minimum effort on your part.

Those numbers are double if you invest the maximum contribution allowed ($204,000-$720,000). This type of money will assure you that you won't be relying solely on social security when you retire.

You would now have financial security.

By using these retirement instruments, you are taking advantage of the best wealth-building system in the world for workers. When used correctly, you could amass a fortune in a small amount of time as a worker. I have seen workers with seven-figure accounts after 25 years of investing in IRAs/401k programs.

Those monies allowed them to retire multi-millionaires, all because they consistently contributed to these instruments. And you can do the same. It's not out of your reach.

This is true, regardless of what your age may be. Even if you are 55 years old and don't see yourself retiring for another 15 years, you could still benefit from this process. You would probably want to make the maximum contribution to get the full benefit.

Most importantly, you won't be depending only on Social Security. That's a good thing. And, if you are younger, you could become a multi-millionaire before you reach 50.

Automatic withdrawals can make this a reality. It's an easy and straightforward process. There's no need to remember if you sent in a contribution or whether you have the money to invest. It's a set-and-leave-type approach. With this type of withdrawal, you determine how much to save from your check or account.

You can always increase or decrease the amount that you are contributing and the type of investments that you are making. That flexibility gives you total control over the account. Thus, you determine how fast your wealth accumulates.

The key to this approach is to stay consistent with the withdrawal, regardless of the amount. Just keep the investing going. Eventually, you will have a sizable balance. No longer will the fear of retiring be a concern to you. You will be financially secure and able to live your life to the fullest.

Plan #2 Life Insurance Investing

Yes, life insurance is a great investment vehicle. It's arguably the best instrument to put your monies. You will have to stop thinking of this instrument as a death benefit and instead see it as a life asset. Any type of life insurance is suitable for your investment portfolio. But for this plan, I'm talking about either whole life or universal life.

Remember, you will need to consult an insurance agent to get the right type of policy for your needs.

The reason for my focus on these types of insurance is that they both offer a cash-value component. They provide you with access to cash if you need it. You can access that cash tax-free, in most cases.

That's in conjunction with the death benefit to your beneficiaries. Also, life insurance is not taxed when it is distributed to your heirs, and it doesn't go to probate. These are benefits that can't be ignored.

Especially if you are building wealth for your family, there's no other investment that provides that type of protection for your beneficiaries. With a life insurance policy, you get to deliver wealth for yourself and your family into posterity.

Getting a life insurance policy is easy, but I would avoid buying those television plans. Use a broker. A broker can help you access a variety of options. They can help you decide which is better, whole life or universal life.

You should have the premiums deducted automatically—another automatic withdrawal scenario—because you don't want to miss a payment and allow the policy to lapse.

I have heard of that happening several times. So, use an automatic withdrawal to avoid that.

Here's what happens after five years of owning the policy. You will now have some cash value. That's money you can use for a myriad of things. The good part is that you will be able to access the principal part of that cash tax-free.

This is unlike an IRA/401(k), where you would have to pay the penalty. If you are under 59.5, that's a great benefit, and another reason to have this instrument in your portfolio.

If you are going to retire and need supplemental income, this policy can provide it via its cash value component. Upon your death, the balance in the account goes to your beneficiaries without probate or taxes, providing your loved ones with the financial security you desired.

For example, if you get a whole life policy worth $250,000, after five years, you may have a cash surrender value of $30,000. You now have $30,000 available to you. Then, the balance of $220,000 is what your beneficiaries would receive upon your death.

That's a win/win scenario. Also, it is how wealth accumulates, and people become more prosperous by using this instrument to strengthen their assets. You should do the same. It's a secure investment to make, and the benefits are many. Please consult an insurance agent before investing in a policy. But make sure you get a plan asap. You will thank yourself later.

Plan #3 Mutual Fund Investing

If you are interested in stock investing, but you don't know how or have the time to learn how, then you may want to consider investing in mutual funds that fit your investment goal. It's the easiest way to get involved with stocks, without having to stress about whether you picked a winner or loser.

There are 9356 mutual funds in the USA, according to Statista. Don't let that number scare you. It's not difficult finding one that fits your needs. There's an unlimited number of sites willing to help you find mutual funds. The most important things to sort by are expense ratio and the 10-year average return historical figures.

Expense ratios are significant because that's what you are paying to invest in that fund. Expense ratios can go from .09 percent for passive managed to .78 for actively managed funds, on average.

Just remember: the lower the expense ratio, the better for your net returns from that fund. And index funds offer some of the lowest expense ratios. It's passively managed.

The reason you are looking at the 10-year historical returns is that you want to see what it does over an extended period, which is how long you should be looking to have that account.

Mutual funds, just like most investments, are suitable for long-term holding. Jumping in and out of mutual funds isn't going to make you any money. So, think long-term when investing in this instrument.

Now the best way to do this is to use automatic withdrawals. This way will allow you to stay invested during good and bad times. Because it allows you to capture more equity when the net asset value is low during bad times, it's sort of like benefiting from a stock split. If you can keep yourself invested in 10 years or better, you will have a sizable amount of money in this asset.

For example, let's say you find a growth fund that has been yielding a 10% average yearly return. And, you invest the minimum, in most cases $1,000, to open the account. With that, you set up an automatic withdrawal of $300 monthly; you can always increase or decrease that amount.

But I have found that to be a manageable amount of money not to miss from the budget. After 10 years, you would have saved $36,000; and with a 10% yearly interest, that amount would be $60,000. That's a lot of money!

Now, imagine that account growing like that for 20-30 years. With the automatic withdrawals, it's like you are investing out of sight because you aren't actively involved with the investment.

Even though it's accumulating riches, your investing is active while you are passive. That's the ultimate type of investing. You should find a mutual fund that fits your needs and set up this plan. Allow it to grow uninterrupted for a few years.

Keep It Simple, Stupid

The plans listed have been proven to make people financially secure, primarily working people. I have and still use all three of these plans to increase my wealth. These are simple approaches to getting wealthy.

You don't have to use a lot of effort to make these investments successful. You need to do it.

Ideally, you should do all three because it will help you increase your wealth astronomically. But if you can't do all three, then you most definitely should get life insurance and an IRA/401(k).

These two are necessary if you are a working person with a family. The benefits of having them far outweigh the cost. And, by using automatic withdrawals, you don't have to keep reminding yourself of when to invest, and the amount invested stays consistent.

Most importantly, you are using the "out of sight, out of mind" approach to investing. This approach will significantly help you build wealth, especially if you are a heavy consumer.

Now, here are some examples of how fast you can accumulate money using these three instruments:

After ten years of investing maximum amounts:

A 401(k) account would have $190,000/$250,000, excluding interest gained. Remember, always fund your 401(k) before you spend anywhere else, other than on a personal residence. So, if you can only invest about $10,000 yearly, that's OK. Something is better than nothing.

An IRA account would have $60,000/$70,000, excluding interest gained, if you don't have access to a 401(k). You must use this instrument. It'll give you the same tax benefits as well as a source of money to use for other investments, such as your primary home.

A whole/universal life insurance policy for $250,000, depending on age and the specific plan, could give you an additional $30,000 in cash value after having the policy for only five years. (Always consult with an insurance broker.)

You must use these investments to get rich. They were created to help working people build wealth. There are no better investments to make if you are a working person. Even buying a house doesn't offer the same tax benefits.

Using these investments will make your net worth soar.

The 2014 census bureau survey found the median net worth in the USA was $74,000, and the median retirement account value was $46,000. As you can see from the example above, you would, after ten years, have an above-average net worth and account value.

It's very doable.

When you have the funds automatically withdrawn, that's the key to this investing. Stay consistently invested. That'll allow it to accumulate faster. These monies will benefit you throughout your life, whether via taxes, distributions, or supplementing your SSI.

These monies can also be used to create more wealth by investing in other opportunities that may arise.

Many have used these accounts to get extremely rich, whether they invested in real estate, business opportunities, or stocks, all of which are allowed with retirement funds. That's another benefit to using these vehicles to build wealth.

Keep in mind the key to building wealth is to have a workable plan. It helps if that plan provides you with the benefits that these instruments offer, and it behooves you to use these accounts in your wealth-building strategy.

Before you use these funds for other investments, try to stay invested for a minimum of ten years unless it's your primary residence. You will be glad you did it. You are guaranteed to help your financial future.

Chapter Review

- Invest in your 401(k) before any other asset, outside of a primary home.
- After five years, your whole/universal life insurance will have equity.
- Mutual funds are great for building long-term wealth.
- Use these instruments to get rich. They are proven.

CONCLUSION

Thanks for reading this book. And, I hope this information provided you with a new way of thinking about getting rich. These investments were created to help the working person obtain the American Dream. If used correctly, these investments will make your money grow. Ultimately, creating a fortune for you and your family.

This book was edited and proofread electronically and by humans to ensure a quality written product. But there still may be some grammatical errors that were missed in the process. If you do find any errors, please, let me know at clyde@yourcpatax.com

Please, share your thoughts in a Review. Any feedback is greatly appreciated, and thank you again, for reading this book.

Disclaimer

The information provided herein by the author is provided "as is". Use this information at your own risk. The publisher/author is not a licensed insurance agent or financial planner. You should always consult a professional before investing. The publisher/author disclaim any liabilities for any losses or personal damages resulting from the information in this book.

Copyright

.